FISHING LOGBOOK

FOR KIDS

OBSERVE AND RECORD YOUR CATCHES

DAVID LISI

ROCKRIDGE
PRESS

I would like to dedicate this book to all new anglers.
May you find as much joy in fishing as I have.

Series Designer: Kristine Brogno
Interior and Cover Designer: Jane Archer
Art Producer: Sue Bischofberger and Tom Hood
Editor: Elizabeth Baird
Production Editor: Ruth Sakata Corley
Production Manager: Jose Olivera
Cover and interior illustrations © Bindy James, 2021; Illustrations for *How to Bait a Hook* and *Catch and Release* by Monika Melnychuk; Author photograph courtesy Dominic Lisi

ISBN: Print 978-1-64876-755-5
R0

THE ANGLER'S TACKLE BOX

Welcome, anglers! Ever wonder why some people seem to catch more fish than others? One secret of the world's best anglers is that they write about their fishing trips in journals. They record as much information about their days on the water as they can, even if they don't catch any fish.

They do this because of one important reason—knowing how you caught a fish in the past can help you catch more fish in the future. For example, if you look back at your journal from a windy, cloudy day and see that you used a red lure to catch a fish, you just may want to try a red lure the next time it's windy and cloudy.

In this book, we will cover some basic fishing information to help you become a master angler. We'll then break down all the sections of this journal, with tips on how best to record your fishing expeditions. At the end of the book, you'll find a Life List, where you can write down all your most memorable catches. Let's get started!

KNOTS TO KNOW

Knots are the most important connection (aside from your line) between you and the fish. Weak or improperly tied knots break easily and can even untie while you're fishing. The last thing you want is to lose out on the fish of a lifetime because of a bad knot.

Each of the knots listed below can be used for other applications, but will work best for the specific reason laid out. Be sure to practice these knots often. It can be hard to remember them when you are on the water fishing. An easy way to practice at home is with a round shoelace or twine.

THE IMPROVED CLINCH KNOT

The improved clinch knot, or cinch knot, is great for tying your line to a hook or lure. Here's how to tie it.

1. Run the tag end (shorter end) of your fishing line through the hook eye, leaving about 6 or 8 inches of line.

2. Take the tag end and wind it onto the standing line about 5 to 7 times, leaving a loop in the line near the hook eye.

IMPROVED CLINCH KNOT INSTRUCTIONS

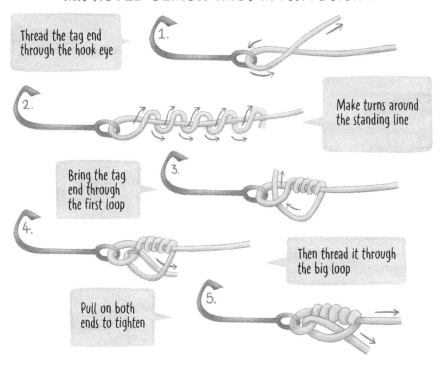

Thread the tag end through the hook eye

1.

2.

Make turns around the standing line

Bring the tag end through the first loop

3.

4.

Then thread it through the big loop

Pull on both ends to tighten

5.

3. Run the tag end back through the loop you left at the ring eye of the hook.

4. Run the tag end through the second loop you created after step 3.

5. Pull the tag end along with the standing line and the knot will begin to tighten.

6. Pull the standing line away from your hook, tightening the knot.

7. Trim your tag end close to the knot.

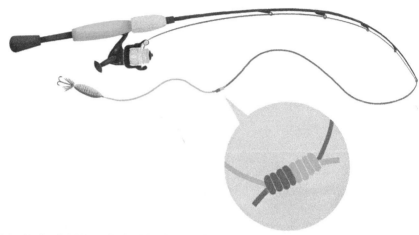

THE DOUBLE UNI KNOT

The double uni knot is great for tying two different fishing lines together, like tying a leader line to your main line. Here's how to tie it.

1. Lay the ends of your two lines next to each other, overlapping by several inches.

2. Peel one end back and wrap it around both lines 3 or 4 times, then through the loop that formed when you doubled back. Pull on the tag end to tighten. You now have one uni knot.

3. Repeat step 2 with the other line. This is your second uni knot.

4. Pull the two standing ends in opposite direction to tighten. The two knots should slide toward each other and eventually meet.

5. Trim the tag ends off.

DOUBLE UNI KNOT

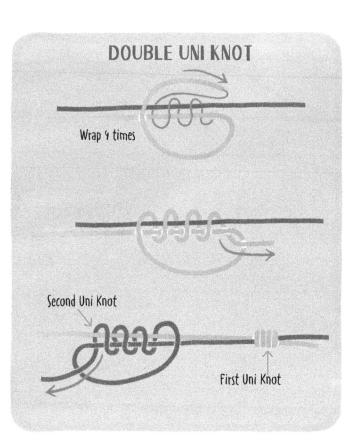

Wrap 4 times

Second Uni Knot

First Uni Knot

PULL LINES TO TIGHTEN KNOT

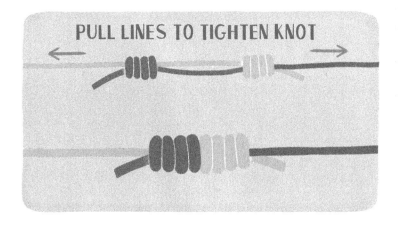

THE ARBOR KNOT

The arbor knot is most commonly used for tying your fishing line to your reel. Here's how to tie it.

1. Wrap the end of your line around the spool of the reel.

2. Tie a simple overhand knot with the tag end around the standing end of the line.

3. Tie a second overhand knot on the tag end of the line about an inch or two from the first overhand knot.

Wrap fishing line around the main line

4. Pull the standing end of the line. This will slide the first overhand knot down to the spool. It will also cause the second overhand knot to jam against the first.

5. Trim any excess line. Congratulations! You've just securely attached new line to your fishing reel.

Tie an overhand knot around the
main line and tighten the knot

Tie another overhand
knot with the tag end.

Pull the main line to move the two
knots together against the reel.

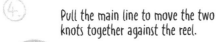

DO I NEED A FISHING LICENSE?

Fishing licenses are a great source of funding for the upkeep of fish and their habitats in many states. Purchasing a fishing license can help protect the outdoors for you and others to enjoy for years to come. In most states, if you are 16 years or older, you will have to purchase a fishing license. If you are under 16, you will not need one, but be sure to check your state's regulations and the regulations of private fishing facilities in your area. In some states, you need special "stamps" in order to target certain species, like trout and salmon. Always check and obey local regulations prior to fishing.

HOW TO BAIT A HOOK

It's important to properly bait your hook with live bait or lures. Keeping your bait or lure in the water for as long as possible will give you the best chance of catching a fish, so you want to make sure it's secure and won't fall off in the water. Live earthworms or night crawlers under a bobber are the most common type of bait for beginning anglers. Here are step-by-step instructions for placing a worm securely on a hook.

1. Grab your hook and worm (make sure your hook is tied to your fishing line using an improved clinch knot first—see Knots to Know). Stick the barbed end of the hook into one end of the worm so that it passes all the way through the worm. Be careful not to poke yourself!

2. Push the worm toward the top of the hook, where the hook eye is.

3. Grab the long end of the worm and push it through the hook again, leaving some slack in the loop of the worm's body. Repeat this step with the rest of the worm (3 to 5 times should be enough).

4. Leave a little of the worm's length "limp" at the end to allow it to wiggle and catch a fish's attention.

🦺 SAFETY TIP

Fishing hooks are quite sharp and dangerous, especially when they have a barb. Always have an adult help you bait your hook or tie on a lure with sharp hooks when you first start learning how to fish.

CATCH AND RELEASE

Learning how to release the fish you catch is an important skill for any angler. In fact, the most common thing anglers do after they catch a fish is release it. Catch and release fishing is becoming more and more popular, and there are even regions around the country that do not allow anglers to keep any fish they catch.

In addition, releasing fish is a great way to make sure that there are fish for future anglers to catch. This practice also helps fish grow to their full potential, keeping the population healthy. It is also important to release fish if you have caught the maximum number of fish you're allowed to catch for the day. Always read your local fishing rules for information on catch limits.

The tackle and gear you use go a long way to ensuring the safe release of fish. Remember, fish are living creatures and will become stressed when you catch and reel them in. It is important to be gentle and take care of them so they can survive. Many anglers choose to use barbless hooks and single hooks, instead of treble hooks, when fishing. Barbless hooks and single hooks are easier to remove from the fish, which limits injury to them and reduces handling time. Anglers also use release nets, which are coated with rubber. This helps protect the fish from losing their important slime layer and scales.

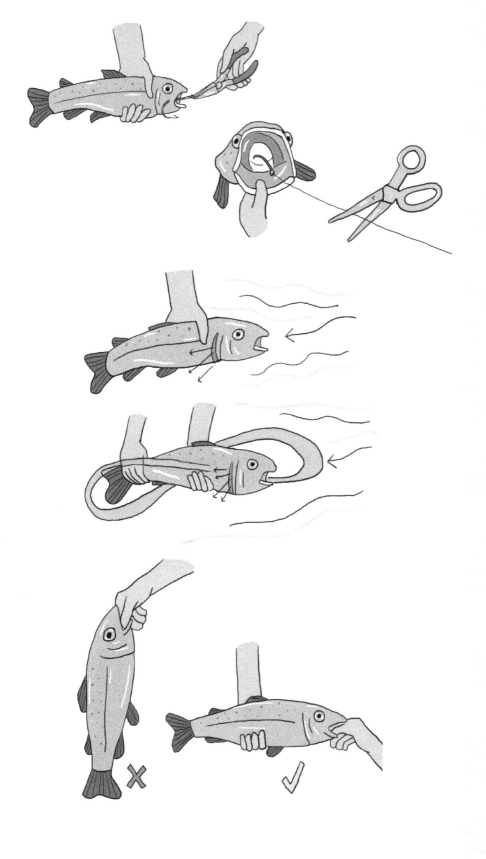

TIPS FOR HANDLING FISH SAFELY

- Use gear that limits stress and damage to fish (barbless or single hooks and a rubber release net).
- Quickly place fish in your net to limit stress. Keep your fish in the water whenever possible.
- Never drag a fish on the rocks or bank. This can injure a fish and also removes the slime layer that protects their skin.
- Always wet your hands before you handle fish to make sure you do not remove their protective slime and scales.
- Never pull a fish out of the net tail-first.
- Remove the hook while the fish is in the net. Be careful, as the fish may thrash, which can cause a hook to catch on your hand or arm.
- Once the hook is removed, gently hold a fish by the tail and support their belly with your opposite hand. Hold them firmly, but do not squeeze the tail and especially do not squeeze the belly and heart. Never grab them by the gills or gill plate.

- If you want to take a picture with the fish, keep the fish in the net and water until someone with a camera is ready. Briefly lift the fish out of the water and snap a couple of quick photos and quickly put the fish back in the water.
- If you are in a river or stream, place the head of the fish upstream so the water can flow through their gills. If you are in a lake or pond, move to a slightly deeper spot and hold the fish until it begins to move and feels ready to be let go. Be sure they swim off under their own power.

HOW TO USE THIS LOGBOOK

In this book, you'll find prompts and pages where you can enter all the most important information about your fishing trips. Check out the next page to see how I filled out my fishing logbook after a great day of winter fly fishing in Alaska.

DATE AND TIME : Monday, February 8, 2021;
9:00 a.m.–4:00 p.m.

LOCATION Kenai River, Cooper Landing, Alaska (south shoreline)

WEATHER: Overcast and cold! About 32 degrees and windy.

FISHING WITH: My friends Felix and Jackie and our dogs Max and Gigi

NOTES: I wasn't sure what to expect on this day of fishing. The weather had been really cold for a few weeks, and there was a lot of ice on the water. But it ended up being a lot of fun! We caught two rainbow trout and one Dolly Varden using flesh flies. Gigi jumped out of the boat trying to catch a fish that Jackie caught! It was Gigi's first time on the water, and it turns out she's a great swimmer.

 **Fish Fact**

Seahorses are the only fish that actually swim upright.

🐟 CATCHES

FISH	LENGTH	WEIGHT	LURE/BAIT USED
RAINBOW TROUT	21 IN	2 LBS.	FLESH FLY (FLY FISHING)
DOLLY VARDEN	13 IN	1 LB.	FLESH FLY (FLY FISHING)
RAINBOW TROUT	25 IN	7 LBS.	FLESH FLY (FLY FISHING)

MY SKETCH

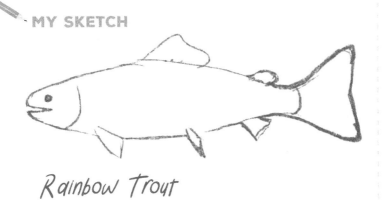

Rainbow Trout

DATE AND TIME

Here you will list the date and time when you went fishing. This information can help you understand the best time of year or time of day to catch certain fish. I'll never forget my first really big rainbow trout. I caught it on February 21, 2018, at noon, and it was 18 degrees out. Every February, I hope to catch another monster!

LOCATION

Write down the location where you fished. It is a good idea to include both general information such as the name of the lake you fished and the state you were in, as well as specific information about where you actually fished. The location or name of the shoreline you fished from, for example, is great to note.

WEATHER

Take notes on the temperature. Even if you don't know the exact temperature, take a good guess. Was it warm, cold, windy, cloudy, or rainy? Fishing in different weather can give you a great idea of how fish respond to different temperatures and conditions.

FISHING WITH OTHERS

Whom did you fish with on this day? Write down their names. Even if you fished alone, be sure to make a note of that (always let an adult know where you will be and when you plan on returning home).

NOTES

It helps to write as many details as possible in this section. You may want to list the gear and tackle you used, and any details about the water temperature or depth. Don't forget to write down any funny or memorable moments you experienced! Some other helpful things to note are:

- What rod and reel combo did you use?
- What lure or bait did you use?
- Did you catch any fish?
- Did you lose any fish you may have had on your line?
- If you caught a fish, where did you catch it? What did it look like?
- Did you try lots of different techniques or stick to the same lure or bait?

FISH FACTS AND TIPS

Scattered throughout the journal are fun facts about fish, as well as some useful fishing tips. Use these to learn more about fish and fishing and amaze your friends and family with your knowledge!

CATCHES

Record all of your catches for the day in this helpful chart. You will want to be sure you write down the length and weight of the fish you caught and what bait, lure, or fly you used to catch that particular fish.

MY SKETCH

You don't have to be a great artist to sketch the fish you see or catch—just give it your best shot! Drawing the shapes, colors, and unique characteristics of the fish you see can help you identify what you saw later when you get home. You can also draw features of the landscape around you to help you map out and identify the best fishing spots.

 **STAYING SAFE**

One of the best ways to make sure that you have a great day on the water is to stay safe. Always let an adult know where you are going fishing for the day and when you plan to come back. Whenever possible, fish with friends or family members.

While fishing is generally a safe sport, some fishing spots can be slippery or have deep holes or fast water. Always be aware of your surroundings. Be cautious with moving water and water where you cannot see the bottom. Never rush when wading in lakes, rivers, streams, or reservoirs.

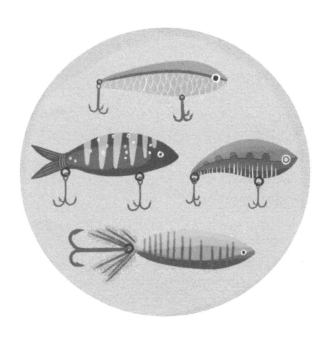

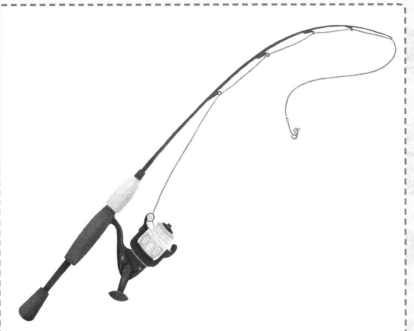

YOUR FISHING LOGBOOK

Here's where you'll record all your fishing adventures. Even if you don't catch anything on a particular outing, be sure to record what the weather was like, whom you fished with, what gear you used, and some memorable moments from the day. Every bit of information you write down will help you achieve future success as an angler.

🕐 **DATE AND TIME:** Aug. 2, 2021

📍 **LOCATION:** 8:30 am - 3:05 pm

☀ **WEATHER:** sunny/windy,

🎣 **FISHING WITH:** Myself, My Grandpa, My 2 Cousins And My Great uncle.

🐟 **NOTES:** I was hoping to AT LEAST catch a perch, but I caught a p-p-Pike!

🎣 **Fishing Tip**

If you do not have a measuring tape with which to measure a fish, you can lay the fish alongside your net or your rod. Mark various lengths on your net or rod at home before you head out for the day. Use small pieces of tape along the length of your rod or net to mark 5, 10, 15, 20, 25 inches, and so on.

 **CATCHES**

FISH	LENGTH	WEIGHT	LURE/BAIT USED
Perch	11 IN	3½ LBS	Night crawler
Rock Bass	9 IN	1⅓ LBS.	Rain worm
Rock Bass	16 IN	5 LBS.	Earth worm
Baby Pike	3 feet	11 LBS.	??? worm

MY SKETCH

Pike

DATE AND TIME:

LOCATION:

WEATHER:

FISHING WITH:

NOTES:

CATCHES

FISH	LENGTH	WEIGHT	LURE / BAIT USED

MY SKETCH

DATE AND TIME:

LOCATION:

WEATHER:

FISHING WITH:

 **NOTES:**

🎣 **Fish Fact**

The scales of a fish grow rings each year. These rings look a bit like the rings on a tree. The scales are a great way for biologists to figure out how old or young a fish is and also show times when the fish grew rapidly or slowly.

CATCHES

FISH	LENGTH	WEIGHT	LURE/BAIT USED

MY SKETCH

DATE AND TIME: ....

LOCATION: ....

....

WEATHER: ....

....

FISHING WITH: ....

....

NOTES: ....

....

....

....

....

....

....

....

....

....

....

....

CATCHES

FISH	LENGTH	WEIGHT	LURE/BAIT USED

MY SKETCH

⏰ **DATE AND TIME:** ....

📍 **LOCATION:** ....

....

🌞 **WEATHER:** ....

🎣 **FISHING WITH:** ....

....

 **NOTES:** ....

....

....

....

....

....

....

🎣 **Fish Fact**

The biggest fish in the world is the giant whale shark. Whale sharks can grow up to 40 feet long and weigh an astonishing 40 tons! They are very gentle and eat plankton—tiny plants and animals that float in water—unlike many of their shark cousins.

CATCHES

FISH	LENGTH	WEIGHT	LURE/BAIT USED

MY SKETCH

DATE AND TIME:

LOCATION:

WEATHER:

FISHING WITH:

NOTES:

CATCHES

FISH	LENGTH	WEIGHT	LURE/BAIT USED

MY SKETCH

DATE AND TIME:

LOCATION:

WEATHER:

FISHING WITH:

NOTES:

Fish Fact

The smallest fish in the world is only a few milli-meters in length. The dwarf minnow lives in forest swamps in Southeast Asia. The water it lives in is very warm and has very low levels of oxygen and high levels of acidity. This environment causes many fish species in the *Paedocypris* genus of fish to have stunted or incomplete growth.

CATCHES

FISH	LENGTH	WEIGHT	LURE/BAIT USED

MY SKETCH

DATE AND TIME: _____

LOCATION: _____
_____

WEATHER: _____

_____
FISHING WITH: _____

_____
NOTES: _____

_____
_____
_____
_____
_____
_____
_____
_____
_____
_____
_____

🐟 CATCHES

FISH	LENGTH	WEIGHT	LURE/BAIT USED

✏ MY SKETCH

DATE AND TIME: ....

LOCATION: ....

....

WEATHER: ....

....

FISHING WITH: ....

....

NOTES: ....

....

....

....

....

....

....

🎣 Fishing Tip

Keep your lures, hooks, flies, and other fishing tackle dry to prevent rusting. You should make sure that everything in your tackle box is clean and dry after each fishing trip. This will make sure that your gear lasts for a long time.

CATCHES

FISH	LENGTH	WEIGHT	LURE/BAIT USED

MY SKETCH

DATE AND TIME: ....

LOCATION: ....

....

WEATHER: ....

....

FISHING WITH: ....

....

NOTES: ....

....

....

....

....

....

....

....

....

Fish Fact

Trout don't have eyelids! They can't close their eyes, so they don't like bright sunlight. If it's sunny out, they're either going to dive deep or look for shade.

CATCHES

FISH	LENGTH	WEIGHT	LURE/BAIT USED

MY SKETCH

DATE AND TIME: ....

LOCATION: ....
....

WEATHER: ....

FISHING WITH: ....
....

NOTES: ....

....
....
....
....
....
....
....
....

🎣 Fish Fact

There are approximately 32,000 species of fish in the world, and scientists are discovering new species all the time.

CATCHES

FISH	LENGTH	WEIGHT	LURE / BAIT USED

MY SKETCH

🕐 **DATE AND TIME:** ....

📍 **LOCATION:** ....

....

☀️ **WEATHER:** ....

🎣 **FISHING WITH:** ....

....

🐟 **NOTES:** ....

....

....

....

....

....

....

....

....

....

....

CATCHES

FISH	LENGTH	WEIGHT	LURE / BAIT USED

MY SKETCH

DATE AND TIME:

LOCATION:

WEATHER:

FISHING WITH:

NOTES:

Fish Fact

Mudskippers are a type of fish that can live on land. In fact, they spend most of their lives on land. They use their fins to crawl around and they even store water in their gills and breathe through their skin.

🐟 CATCHES

FISH	LENGTH	WEIGHT	LURE/BAIT USED

✏️ MY SKETCH

DATE AND TIME: _____

LOCATION: _____

_____

WEATHER: _____

_____

FISHING WITH: _____

_____

NOTES: _____

_____

_____

_____

_____

_____

_____

_____

_____

_____

_____

_____

CATCHES

FISH	LENGTH	WEIGHT	LURE/BAIT USED

MY SKETCH

DATE AND TIME:

LOCATION:

WEATHER:

FISHING WITH:

NOTES:

🎣 **Fishing Tip**

When fishing in cold weather, be sure to dress in layers. It is also a great idea to wear waterproof pants and a rain jacket for added protection.

CATCHES

FISH	LENGTH	WEIGHT	LURE / BAIT USED

MY SKETCH

DATE AND TIME: ....

LOCATION: ....

....

WEATHER: ....

FISHING WITH: ....

....

NOTES: ....

....

....

....

....

....

....

....

....

....

....

....

🐟 CATCHES

FISH	LENGTH	WEIGHT	LURE / BAIT USED

MY SKETCH

DATE AND TIME: ....

LOCATION: ....

....

WEATHER: ....

....

FISHING WITH: ....

....

NOTES: ....

....

....

....

....

....

....

....

....

....

....

....

CATCHES

FISH	LENGTH	WEIGHT	LURE/BAIT USED

MY SKETCH

DATE AND TIME:

LOCATION:

WEATHER:

FISHING WITH:

NOTES:

 **Fish Fact**

Catfish have over 27,000 taste buds. Compare that to humans, who only have 7,000. No wonder they love stinky baits!

CATCHES

FISH	LENGTH	WEIGHT	LURE / BAIT USED

MY SKETCH

DATE AND TIME:

LOCATION:

WEATHER:

FISHING WITH:

NOTES:

CATCHES

FISH	LENGTH	WEIGHT	LURE/BAIT USED

MY SKETCH

DATE AND TIME: ....

LOCATION: ....

....

WEATHER: ....

....

FISHING WITH: ....

 **NOTES:** ....

Fish Fact

Not all fish have scales. Fish like sharks have rough skin, which feels a lot like sandpaper.

CATCHES

FISH	LENGTH	WEIGHT	LURE / BAIT USED

MY SKETCH

DATE AND TIME: ....

LOCATION: ....

....

WEATHER: ....

....

FISHING WITH: ....

....

NOTES: ....

....

....

....

....

....

....

....

....

....

....

🐟 CATCHES

FISH	LENGTH	WEIGHT	LURE / BAIT USED

✏️ MY SKETCH

DATE AND TIME: _____

LOCATION: _____
_____

WEATHER: _____
_____

FISHING WITH: _____
_____

 **NOTES:** _____
_____
_____
_____
_____
_____
_____

🎣 **Fishing Tip**

When recording your catches, make a note of your confidence level. If you believe you will catch a fish, sometimes that can make the difference between catching one and not.

CATCHES

FISH	LENGTH	WEIGHT	LURE/BAIT USED

MY SKETCH

DATE AND TIME: _____

LOCATION: _____

_____

WEATHER: _____

_____

FISHING WITH: _____

_____

NOTES: _____

_____

_____

_____

_____

_____

_____

_____

_____

_____

_____

CATCHES

FISH	LENGTH	WEIGHT	LURE/BAIT USED

MY SKETCH

🕐 DATE AND TIME: ....

📍 LOCATION: ....

....

☀ WEATHER: ....

....

🎣 FISHING WITH: ....

....

🐟 NOTES: ....

....

....

....

....

....

....

....

....

....

🎣 Fish Fact

A person who studies fish is called an "ichthyologist".

CATCHES

FISH	LENGTH	WEIGHT	LURE / BAIT USED

MY SKETCH

🕐 **DATE AND TIME:** ....

📍 **LOCATION:** ....

....

🌞 **WEATHER:** ....

....

🎣 **FISHING WITH:** ....

 NOTES: ....

🎣 **Fish Fact**

Fish have a "lateral line" along their sides. This is
a line of special scales that run from their mouth,
around their eye, then down to their tail. These
scales can help them navigate, sense when there is
wounded prey, and even alert them to danger.

CATCHES

FISH	LENGTH	WEIGHT	LURE/BAIT USED

MY SKETCH

🕐 **DATE AND TIME:** --

📍 **LOCATION:** ---

☀️ **WEATHER:** --

🎣 **FISHING WITH:** ---

🐟 **NOTES:** ---

 Fish Fact

Most fish are cold-blooded. This means that as the temperature of the water changes, so does their body temperature. Often, when water warms up slightly after it has been cold, it can cause fish to feed and be very active. This is a great time to go fishing!

CATCHES

FISH	LENGTH	WEIGHT	LURE/BAIT USED

MY SKETCH

DATE AND TIME:

LOCATION:

WEATHER:

FISHING WITH:

NOTES:

Fishing Tip

Don't forget to bring some snacks and drinks whenever you head out fishing. It is important to stay hydrated and have lots of energy for a long day on the water. Be sure never to litter. Always pack out what you pack in.

🐟 CATCHES

FISH	LENGTH	WEIGHT	LURE/BAIT USED

✏ MY SKETCH

🕐📅 DATE AND TIME: _____

📍 LOCATION: _____
_____

☀️ WEATHER: _____

🎣 FISHING WITH: _____

_____

🐟 NOTES: _____

_____

_____

_____

_____

_____

_____

_____

_____

🎣 Fish Fact

Tuna are speedy fish. They can swim up to 43 miles per hour. That's faster than the speed limit of most towns!

🐟 CATCHES

FISH	LENGTH	WEIGHT	LURE/BAIT USED

✏️ MY SKETCH

⏰ **DATE AND TIME:** ....

📍 **LOCATION:** ....
....

☀️ **WEATHER:** ....

🎣 **FISHING WITH:** ....
....

🐟 **NOTES:** ....
....
....
....
....
....

🎣 Fish Fact

According to the *Guinness Book of World Records*,
the world's longest fishing rod measures an incredible 73 feet 7 inches! It was made by Schweizerischer
Fischereiverband of Switzerland. Can it catch
a fish? Probably not, but it is quite an amazing
accomplishment!

CATCHES

FISH	LENGTH	WEIGHT	LURE/BAIT USED

MY SKETCH

DATE AND TIME:

LOCATION:

WEATHER:

FISHING WITH:

 **NOTES:**

🎣 **Fishing Tip**

One of the best lures that catches fish all over the world is the spoon—an oblong, metal lure named for its resemblance to the bowl of a spoon. The simple design seems to attract fish by reflecting light and moving like prey. These lures date all the way back to the eighth century, when Nordic people began using spoon lures made from local metals.

CATCHES

FISH	LENGTH	WEIGHT	LURE / BAIT USED

MY SKETCH

DATE AND TIME:

LOCATION:

WEATHER:

FISHING WITH:

NOTES:

🎣 Fish Fact

A lot of fish lay eggs, but fish like great white sharks give birth to live babies called pups.

CATCHES

FISH	LENGTH	WEIGHT	LURE/BAIT USED

MY SKETCH

DATE AND TIME: ....

LOCATION: ....
....

WEATHER: ....

....

FISHING WITH: ....

....

NOTES: ....

....

....

....

....

....

....

....

🎣 Fishing Tip

Most fish can see color. Their eyes adapt to the particular environment they live in. Sometimes changing from one color lure to another can help you catch a fish, even if you use the same type of lure, bait, or fly.

CATCHES

FISH	LENGTH	WEIGHT	LURE/BAIT USED

MY SKETCH

DATE AND TIME: _____

LOCATION: _____
_____

WEATHER: _____

FISHING WITH: _____
_____

NOTES: _____
_____
_____
_____
_____
_____
_____
_____

 Fish Fact

More people fish in the United States than play golf and tennis combined. An estimated 40 million people fish in the United States. That's a lot of people!

CATCHES

FISH	LENGTH	WEIGHT	LURE / BAIT USED

MY SKETCH

DATE AND TIME:

LOCATION:

WEATHER:

FISHING WITH:

NOTES:

Fish Fact

Some fish actually help keep other fish clean.
These "cleaner" fish remove harmful parasites from
their cousins.

CATCHES

FISH	LENGTH	WEIGHT	LURE/BAIT USED

MY SKETCH

DATE AND TIME:

LOCATION:

WEATHER:

FISHING WITH:

NOTES:

🎣 **Fish Fact**

Some fish, such as the batfish, will play dead when danger is near. They will lie flat on the surface until a predator leaves the area.

CATCHES

FISH	LENGTH	WEIGHT	LURE / BAIT USED

MY SKETCH

DATE AND TIME: ....

LOCATION: ....
....

WEATHER: ....

....
FISHING WITH: ....

....
NOTES: ....

....

....

....

....

....

....

....

🎣 Fishing Tip

Always respect and treat your fellow anglers kindly.
If someone is fishing in your favorite spot, you can
either move on or ask permission to fish together.

CATCHES

FISH	LENGTH	WEIGHT	LURE/BAIT USED

MY SKETCH

LIFE LIST

Your life list is a place to record the most memorable fish you've ever caught. You can list the biggest fish you've caught, your first catch of a particular species, a catch that has unique markings, or even one with an incredible story about how you caught it. There will be many highlights from your fishing career that you will want to remember, so be sure to write them down.

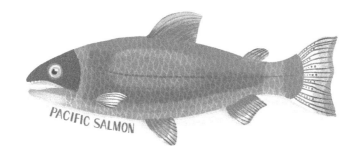

PACIFIC SALMON

DATE	TYPE OF FISH
1.	
2.	
3.	
4.	
5.	
6.	
7.	
8.	
9.	
10.	
11.	
12.	
13.	
14.	
15.	
16.	
17.	
18.	
19.	
20.	

DATE	TYPE OF FISH
21.	
22.	
23.	
24.	
25.	
26.	
27.	
28.	
29.	
30.	
31.	
32.	
33.	
34.	
35.	
36.	
37.	
38.	
39.	
40.	

DATE	TYPE OF FISH
41. _____	_____
42. _____	_____
43. _____	_____
44. _____	_____
45. _____	_____
46. _____	_____
47. _____	_____
48. _____	_____
49. _____	_____
50. _____	_____
51. _____	_____
52. _____	_____
53. _____	_____
54. _____	_____
55. _____	_____
56. _____	_____
57. _____	_____
58. _____	_____
59. _____	_____
60. _____	_____

About the Author

David Lisi is a lifelong angler who owns a fishing guide and outfitter business on the Kenai Peninsula in Alaska. Fishing has always been a part of David's life. Some of his earliest memories are of him fishing in diapers with his family at a lake in upstate New York.

He spent most of his youth exploring the rivers and lakes near his hometown. Eventually, he made his way to Alaska where he now lives. He takes people from all over the world fishing on the world-famous Kenai River for rainbow trout, Dolly Varden trout, and Pacific salmon.

Not a day goes by that he isn't fishing or thinking about fishing!